MW00723425

To:

From:

A ZOMBIE'S
Guide to the Holidays

It's a Wonderful Afterlife!

By Ruth Cullen
Illustrated by Lisa Fargo

PETER PAUPER PRESS, INC.
White Plains, New York

Deadication

To my family, friends, colleagues, and neighbors . . . I could eat you up.

—R.C.

Illustrations © Lisa Fargo
Designed by Heather Zschock

Copyright © 2011
Peter Pauper Press, Inc.
202 Mamaroneck Avenue
White Plains, NY 10601
All rights reserved
ISBN 978-1-4413-0613-5
Printed in China
7 6 5 4 3 2 1

Visit us at www.peterpauper.com

A ZOMBIE'S
Guide to the Holidays

Introduction
It's the most wonderful time of the year.

Zombies, it just doesn't get any better than the holiday season—the silent nights, mistletoe moments, **warm hearts...**

Consider it all a special gift to you—unsuspecting holiday carolers, crowded shopping malls, and Humans who have had one too many egg noggins at the neighborhood open house. **Happy Holidays!**

Let this book be your guide to surviving—and thriving—this holiday season. Complete with tips on where to find the best brain food at the mall (NOM NOM NOM), and how to embrace holiday stress, this little handbook will help you ooze happiness from the inside out. You'll also learn when to lend a hand and shake a leg. Most important, you'll be reminded of what really matters during this holiday season and all year round: *Making sure the holiday spirit is infectious.* Perhaps it's a wonderful afterlife after all.

Holiday Stress
Keep Your Head

In the midst of holiday mayhem, keep your head—literally—by staying focused on the task at hand. Don't bite off more than you can chew, but if you do, be discreet or you *will* get caught with a foot in your mouth.

Gnaw Away at Stress

One of the best things about the holidays is that Humans completely lose their minds and then we devour them. It's that simple. Overwhelmed by the pressures of the season, the teeming masses become an all-you-can-eat buffet-o-brains.

Nothing says "Group hug!" like a throng of harried shoppers at the mall. Here are some tips for managing *their* holiday stress:

-  Reach out to those incapacitated by the headaches of the holidays.

- Seek the silent Scrooges stewing about "to do" lists and demands on their time.

- Scout out public seating areas for panicky women and their snoring spouses.

Zom B.

Stressed Out of Their BRAINS
Know the Signs

TYPE	CHARACTERISTIC
Withdrawn ······▶	Engrossed in ···· handheld electronic devices
Hyperactive ·············	
Dazed, Confused ·········▶	Vacant staring at department store window displays

Here's a brief holiday primer on three common types of distracted Mortals.

ZOMBIE APPROACH

Rapid eye movement, flailing arms, running to catch train

→ Full frontal embrace

→ Rear advance

→ Zombie free choice

Remember

Stress Is a Silent Killer

Stress (like you!) eats away at the Living, but use your head and target the introverts suffering from unrealistic expectations and negative self-talk, *not* those overreacting, stomping their feet, and looking for a fight.

Avoid Those Consuming Excess Caffeine and Sugar

Do not linger around hipster coffee houses or cupcake shops during the holidays—you're likely to encounter a sleep-deprived, strung-out shopper who's had one too many espresso lattes. Humans amped on caffeine and sugar can be feisty, combative, and unpredictable.

Stay Cool

Just because you're a Post-Lifer doesn't mean you're immune to stress. Grappling with your food and shambling to keep up with the Horde *will* take a toll on your already decomposing body. Be cool: You don't have to give an arm or a leg while you're taking one.

Repeat after Me:
I am Living Impaired and That's OK.

If at any point during the holiday season you find yourself wedged between a rock and a hard place, remember: You're a Zombie! And everything is going to be A-OK.

SELF-AFFIRMATIONS FOR THE ANXIOUS ZOMBIE

Today is the first day of the rest of my afterlife.

I am different, unique, and special. No one else is exactly like me.

I am joyful. I ooze happiness from the inside out.

I have everything I need, even if I'm missing an appendage or two.

I can handle whatever Life (or Death) throws at me.

Holiday Spirit

It's Infectious

'Tis the season for sharing, and Zombies have a unique opportunity to spread the joy... one Human at a time.

DRESS TO KILL

Don we now our gay apparel... Fa la la la la la...

Choose bold, bright, festive seasonal attire to attract Humans while diverting attention from gaping wounds or anything that might be a "*dead giveaway.*" Remember: Clothes may make the Human, but during the holidays, they *definitely* make the Zombie.

Seasonal Style Tip

 **DO...** choose from these Zombie-approved holiday fashions:

- Bright red, green, or plaid clothing
- Sweaters and vests appliquéd with reindeer, snowmen, and teddy bears
- Santa suits (including hat and beard)
- Elf suits (including tights and boots)
- Yarmulkes
- Reindeer antlers

for Zombies

Don't... risk unnecessary attention by making bad accessory choices, such as:

- Jingle bell shoelaces
- Christmas light necklaces
- Glowing Rudolph noses

Reel in the Holiday Spirit

If your Undead spirit needs a little boost, or if you're simply looking to whet your appetite, look no further than these classic Zombie holiday movies:

It's a Wonderful Afterlife

Mandible on 34th Street

Elf of the Living Dead

How the Zombies Stole Christmas

It's a Very Zombie Christmas

Bait the Halls . . .

Deck the Living

Like moths to a flame, Humans cannot resist the lure of seasonal decor—and neither should you. It can be a truly satisfying experience. While they stand transfixed, enjoying those blinking lights and intriguing inflatables, YOU can enjoy THEM.

Beware Open Flames

Let's face it: Zombies and fire don't really mix. And though candlelight is flattering to festering folk like you, steer clear of any and all open flames, including:

- Candles
- Luminaries
- Fondue pots
- Menorahs
- Yule logs
- Flaming drinks

If You Go a Caroling ...
Lip Sync

Just because your singing days are over doesn't mean you should miss out on jolly evenings in the company of carolers. Especially since they're Living. And it's dark. Try not to moan along. It's a dead giveaway.

Favorite Zombie Christmas Carols

Even the Horde can get a little sentimental during the holidays. Here are a few all-time Zombie classics:

Zombies Are Coming to Town

Gnaw All Ye Faithful

Good Chew Ye Merry Gentlemen

Silent Night, Unholy Night

Santa Zombie

Jingle Braaaiins

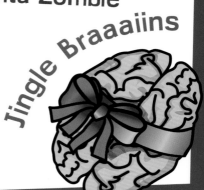

Shopping for Others

During the holidays, there's one destination for Zombies with others in mind: THE MALL. Consider it your own personal "food court."

SHOP TILL THEY DROP

Shopping is the number one pastime of the Living at holiday time, followed by eating, drinking, and standing immobilized in front of screens large and small. The beauty of the mall is that it enables Humans to enjoy all of these favorite activities—while you enjoy yours.

Go with the Flow

Don't be surprised if Horde members confuse you for a Human at the mall, or if you make the same mistake. Most Zombies (except Crawlers) find it easy to blend in with the passing parade of shoppers shuffling from store to store. Shake it off and shamble on.

Get Inside the Minds of Savvy Shoppers

Looking for the best "brain food" at the mall? Set your sights on smart (a.k.a. *brainy*) shoppers, the ones concentrating on their lists and checking them twice. Like them, you will be successful by:

- Making a plan and sticking to it
- Staying focused
- Pacing yourself
- Snacking as you go to keep energy levels high

Midnight Madness

*Save (Or Was that "Savor")
an Arm and a Leg*

Crazy, round-the-clock sales provide opportunities to save even *more* than an arm and a leg. By all means, join the Humans as they wait in line, traverse darkened parking lots, load packages into car trunks, or amble around the mall at 3AM—especially on "Black Friday" when they're fighting off the Thanksgiving tryptophan.

Don't Be a Conspicuous Consumer

Over-indulging at the shopping center will get you noticed for all the wrong reasons. Keep a low profile. Don't dine at the food court. Instead, seek out dressing rooms, restrooms, and elevators where you can have some privacy and, if needed, a new change of clothes.

Avoid the Hard Sell

Steer clear of aggressive sales-people—kiosk vendors, cosmetics counter staff, and anyone working on commission. Unless you can "close a deal" of your own, skip the sales pitches; the risk of exposure is far too great.

Treat Yourself

When you're so focused on others, it's easy to forget about yourself. Take time to visit stores of *your* choice (e.g., *De Kaymart*, *Targets*, *Toes "R" Us*) and pick up practical necessities like these:

- Helmet
- Slip-on clogs
- Perfume or cologne: *Eternity, Obsession, Tabu, or Delicious*
- First aid supplies: Duct tape, fire extinguisher, staple gun
- Oversized sunglasses

Holiday Parties

Wear the Lampshade

No one parties like the Living Dead. *No one.* Suffice it to say, with a Zombie in da house, no one will ever be the same again.

BE THE UN-LIFE OF THE PARTY

Drag yourself if need be, just do whatever it takes to get to the next holiday party this season... and the next, and the next. And leave a *lasting* impression wherever you go.

Party Tips

DO...

- Dress for success with festive attire.
- Arrive fashionably late to allow partygoers time to relax.
- Get acquainted with your surroundings, including bathrooms, coatrooms, and basements.
- Reach out to loners and find ways to connect.
- Have an exit strategy . . . just in case.

Don't...

- 👁 Knock, ring the doorbell, or otherwise overtly announce your presence.

- 👁 Make eye contact with party guests until late into the night.

- 👁 Overlook the opportunity to play bartender and refill guests' glasses.

- 👁 Forget to work the room and the house.

Play Games

When it comes to party games, remember everyone is "game" and no one makes the rules but you. Create your own murder mystery game or "brainteaser." *If four Humans walked into the coatroom but only one walked out, how many brains will I have?* Trust me, playing *Cranium* and *Twist-her* have never been more fun.

Shake a Leg

Never miss an opportunity to hit the dance floor. When the lights go down and the music starts pumping—whether it's "I Will Survive" or "Jingle Bell Rock"—it's time to get your freak on. After all, Zombies *invented* break dancing. (And we're the original head bangers!) So show the Living what it really means to "tear up" the dance floor or "do the twist."

ZOMBIE DANCE MOVES

- Belly dancing
- Break dancing
- Freaking
- Grinding
- Head banging
- Shake, shimmy, and stomp
- Interpretive dance

Dealing with Drunks

Remember: Alcohol has a preservative effect on Zombies, so seek out those slurring, sloshed, and balance-impaired partiers. They'll be putty in your gnarly, outstretched hands after one too many egg noggins. Meanwhile, you'll fit right in with the inebriated and benefit immeasurably from picking their brains.

FAVORITE ZOMBIE SPIRITS

Bloody Mary

Egg Noggin

Fuzzy Navel

Mind Eraser

Zombie (but not Flaming Zombies)

Be Mindful of Mistletoe

Mistletoe provides intriguing opportunities for Zombies and party guests to connect, but before you lumber your way toward something dangling from a doorway, make sure it's mistletoe and not, say, a piñata. If any other kind of "toe" is hanging from the ceiling, you're best advised to move on.

Have an Exit Strategy

Chances are you *will* get caught
red-handed at a party this season.
Before you find yourself cornered
by a close talker or at the wrong
end of a fire poker, make sure you
have a getaway plan. Know where
your exits are, and don't hesitate
to create a diversion.

Family Togetherness

Overcoming
"You're Dead to Me"

For both the Living and Living-Impaired, the holidays mean spending time with family—time to experience the ties that bind, strangle, and suffocate.

No family is perfect, but instead of focusing on what's *wrong* with your Undead family— the mealtime scuffles, lack of communication, hygiene issues—focus on what's *right*. You have a growing Zombie family with whom you can share your heart (and liver and kidney).

Keep the Peace

Here are some helpful tips for a happy Horde this holiday season.

- Lend a hand.
- Keep your mouth shut (unless you're eating).
- Turn a blind eye.

Don't...

- Spill your guts.

- Give others a cold shoulder (warm is better).

- Lose face (if you can help it).

Choose Your Battles

Avoid reopening old wounds without first taking a moment to reflect. Before you rip into someone, ask yourself: Who else is around? Are there any visible weapons? Have I lost my head? It's OK to drag yourself away from some battles and focus on those you know you can win.

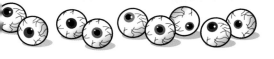

Take a Breather

Humans have family issues, too. In fact, they'll look for any excuse to get out of the house if the relatives are visiting. Don't leave those warm-bodied hosts out in the cold. Be waiting when they venture outside for a walk or jog. While they get some air, you can get them.

Create a Picture Perfect Holiday

Looking for a great photo opportunity? The Living will spend hours trying to capture the perfect Kodak moment for greeting cards, giving you plenty of time to catch them off guard. As they say "Cheese" for the hundredth time and bicker about looking happy, zoom in and take a shot of your own.

Remember:

Blood Is Thicker Than Water

Never underestimate family ties. Humans can show surprising strength and resourcefulness when called on to protect their offspring. Siblings in particular can be powerful foes, drawing from the same well of raw emotions that divides them, and channeling that aggression against you.

Nom Nom Nom
Holiday Eats

YES, ZOMBIE, THERE IS A SANTA CLAUS. AND HE'S DELICIOUS.

Temptations abound during the holidays. Give yourself permission to splurge, no matter if you've been good ... or very, very bad.

EAT SMART

Remember: A healthy, active brain is a tasty one. Visit libraries, bookstores, and museums to find the best holiday fare. Avoid Humans who dine at fast food restaurants, ride motorcycles without helmets, or spend long periods of time in front of the television set.

Expand You

The season provides a cornucopia of opportunities to try different foods from around the world, each with its own unique flavor. The following list may help you select your menu.

American: Fatty

Canadian: Gamey

Chinese: Sweet and sour*

French: Pair with Bordeaux

Palate

Indian: Spicy

Irish: Notes of whiskey**

Italian: Hot-blooded

Mexican: Tough and hot

Russian: Tough and cold**

* Will leave you feeling hungry an hour later
**Have preservative effects

Tips for Holiday

Follow these guidelines to keep your holiday eating in check this season.

DO...

- Dive into meals head first.
- Embrace new foods.
- Be strategic when it comes to eating.

Eating

Don't...

- Fill up on finger foods.
- Bite off more than you can chew.
- Join holiday feasts at carving time.
- Forget that fruitcake can be used as a weapon.

Favorite Zombie Holiday Foods

Want some food for thought?
Whet your appetite with these
Zombie favorites!

STANDING RIB CAGE

LIVER TARTARE

Now bring us some finger pudding, now bring us some finger pudding . . .

STEWED BRAINS

BLOOD PUDDING

LIMBSMEAT PIE

FINGERBREAD

THUMB BALLS

Avoid Mindless Snacking

Be aware of what you're stuffing in your mouth, and how often you're eating. You don't want to gorge yourself on finger foods—a thumb here, a pinky there— when it's brain food you ultimately require. Remember: Your digestive tract ain't what it used to be, and you don't need anything else slowing you down.

FAVORITE ZOMBIE FINGER FOODS
- Pinkies in a blanket
- Deviled eyeballs
- Meatballs (any kind)
- Toe Fritters

BITE THE HAND THAT FEEDS YOU

Be grateful for what you *have* this season, even if it's not exactly what you *want.* No doubt you'll hunger for things outside your grasp. Just don't let that cause you to lose sight of what's right there in front of you.

Holiday Travel Getting Around

I'll be in your home for Christmas, you can count on me . . .

When it comes to holiday travel, the old Zombie credo rings true:

Neither snow nor rain nor heat nor gloom of night (nor windows, doors, and most weapons) will stay the Undead from the completion of their appointed rounds.

Hang with the Horde

It's a good idea to surround yourself with others who look like you—
which may mean everything
from pale, mutilated, lumbering
Staggerers to green, one-eyed,
festering Crawlers. That said, don't
be afraid to take the road less
shambled, particularly if the Hordies
are heading toward an army base,
gun show, or bonfire.

Chew the Ears off Fellow Travelers

During the holidays, Humans spend hours trapped within the confines of train stations, airports, and bus depots, waiting for public transportation that's often delayed. It's a beautiful thing.

Tips for the Undead Pedestrian

DO...

-  Look both ways before you cross a street.

- Heed traffic and pedestrian signals.

- Mind the gap.

Black ice, snow plows, and falling icicles can be problematic for Zombies during the winter months. Here are some suggestions to keep in mind when traveling on foot.

Don't...

- Stagger out into oncoming traffic.

- Jaywalk.

- Take short cuts across construction sites or unfrozen ponds and lakes.

Shamble Through the Snow

Travel by foot, if possible, to best enjoy the gifts of the season. Skulk down snow- and ice-covered byways and discover a seemingly limitless supply of stranded motorists (a.k.a. "meals on wheels"). Lumber through neighborhoods and towns and find a smorgasbord of holiday treats: dog walkers, delivery personnel, carolers, and tasty children playing in the snow.

Travel Tips for the Living-Impaired

- Grab a quick bite before you leave.
- Mask unpleasant odors with perfume, mouthwash, or stick-on air fresheners.
- Wear layers. Peel them off one by one.
- Choose appropriate footwear.
- Cut your losses (dangling appendages will only slow you down).
- Avoid full body scanners.

Beat the Heat

Heat wreaks havoc on Zombies, accelerating the process of decay. If you find yourself in a warm climate, travel at night to avoid daytime heat and direct sunlight. In general, steer clear of radiators, saunas, ovens, and tanning beds.

Pace Yourself

Rushing can lead to unfortunate accidents, most of which are entirely preventable.

Remember: You're a Zombie! You're *oozingly* awesome! And you *will* get wherever you're going, even if you lack a limb or two.

Giving: Lend a Hand, Lend an Arm

"Give me your tired, your poor, your huddled masses ..."

Zombies *always* have others in mind, and at no time is your outward focus more evident than during the holidays.

Be a Secret Santa

Get into the hearts and minds of everyone you encounter this season by giving *unexpected* gifts. Like hugs! And squeezes! Pay surprise visits. Step out from the shadows in a Santa suit, or just lurk quietly by the tree until Christmas morning and leave everyone forever changed.

Reach Out to Those in Need

Don't hesitate to approach Humans
during this magical time of year, especially
those who might welcome a little company.
Make the rounds at a hospital during
visiting hours. Drop by an orphanage,
homeless shelter, or nursing home.
Give of yourself in truly meaningful ways.

Help the Less Fortunate

You may be on your last leg, but there are still ways for you to make a difference in the community:

- Lend an ear or give a hand to a food bank.
- Volunteer at an organ donation center.
- Pick someone's brain at your local library.
- Take a bite out of crime.

Favorite Zombie Holiday Charities

Habitat for Inhumanity

Toes for Tots

The United Decay

Zombies without Borders

The Dead Cross

The Salvation Arm

Save the Children ... for Later

Keep Your Chin Up

All the pressures of the season combined with winter blues, or Seasonal Affective Disorder, can leave the Living overwhelmed, frustrated, and depressed. This makes it all the more crucial for you to set a positive example with chin held high. (And what better position from which to open wide and take a bite?)

Remember:

It's What's Inside That Counts

It's easy to get distracted during the holidays and focus on superficial things instead of what's really important. So don't forget, Zombie, it's what's inside that counts: **BRAAIIINS!**

(Not to mention hearts, livers, kidneys, spleens, gallbladders…)